The Giving Story
Rejoicing in God's Grace

Jeffrey Davis

The Giving Story: Rejoicing in God's Grace

Author: Jeffrey Davis

Published by Austin Brothers Publishing

Keller, Texas

www.austinbrotherspublishing.com

ISBN 978-0-9903477-2-9

This and other books published by Austin Brothers Publishing can be purchased at www.austinbrotherspublishing.com

Printed in the United States of America
2015 — First Edition

Contents

Acknowledgements

The stories in this book come from two viewpoints, Ron's and Jeff's. Over the years Ron Roth and Jeff Davis have encountered many people who reflect the grace of God in their lives. Ron's storytelling is over; he now listens to the great storyteller, Jesus, every moment in heaven. Jeff still listens and gathers from others. If your story resonates with Christian giving, please share it! I can be reached at thegivingstory@gmail.com or visit our webpage - www.thegivingstory.com.

Jeffrey Davis

Introduction

This is a book about grace. Even though it is an enormous subject, this is really a small book. The reason is because it is not an attempt to understand all the theological and practical ramifications of God's grace, but rather an explanation of how grace is an integral part of our giving. The title is "The Giving Story." It could very easily be titled, "The Grace Story."

Perhaps the first person to associate the words "grace" and "giving" was the Apostle Paul. In 2 Corinthians he sets out to describe the Christians of Macedonia and the grace they had experienced. In order to understand grace, he spoke about their giving.

Living in three relatively unknown cities (Thessalonica, Berea, and Philippi) the Macedonians were persecuted Christians. As such, we know they were poor because the world does not persecute the rich. Yet, Paul describes their giving as being generous and beyond expectations.

This great story of giving reminds the Apostle of the greatest example of grace giving–Jesus. He concludes his story of the Macedonian giving with these words – "For you know the grace of our Lord Jesus Christ, that though he was rich, yet for your sakes he became poor, so that you through his poverty might become rich." (2 Corinthians 8:9)

Paul tells the story of the Macedonians' giving, not to encourage them to give more, but to encourage the Corinthians. Earlier, the

Corinthians had promised Paul they were going to give an offering to help believers in Jerusalem. Paul received word they were not giving as promised so he shares the story of the Macedonian believers to inspire them. That is what giving stories do.

The Macedonians had experienced the grace of God expressed through Jesus. As a result they became givers with a great story to tell. Once we experience and understand God's grace, we will also be transformed into givers.

That is what this book is all about.

The Backstory of Grace

God's Story, Grace Always

A lawn sign caught my eye as I entered the drive-through of a fast food restaurant. Normally, I don't pay any attention to them, but there was something different about this one. It was strategically placed to catch my eye. And it did. It was an invitation to donate spare change to the restaurant's non-profit cause. The message contained these words.

"Spare change may come from under your seats.
But really, it's found in your heart."

As I continued on my road trip, the message of that sign bounced around in my brain for the next several hours. It really speaks to the core of why we give as Christians. Any giving decision, and the action that follows, comes from the heart.

We live in a society that promotes the accumulation of possessions, the opposite of giving. It is easy to fall into the trap of accumulating more and more "stuff."

If we focus on things of this world we will have a tough time seeing God's immense love for us. The antidote to accumulating is giving. When we give, we focus on others. Giving also testifies that we are simply managers of what God has given us. Through giving, we reflect God's love. The Bible calls that love "grace."

The beginning of grace

All stories have a beginning, well, except for one, and your story is tied to this story. God's book begins with the phrase, "In the beginning God created the heavens and the earth." Earth began with the creating work of a marvelous God. All things on earth trace their origin to this beginning.

There is another beginning. Let's call it a "Once upon an eternity" beginning. "In the beginning was the Word, and the Word was with God, and the Word was God. He was with God in the beginning" (John 1:1,2). The Word, Jesus Christ, was not only with God, but also was and is true God from the *beginning* of eternity. Before the world was created, God was present. How can this be? We don't know, but faith hears and believes.

The story continues in Genesis 1:26: "Let us make man in *our* image, in *our* likeness" (italics mine). Other sections of the Bible tell us that our God is actually three persons in one: Father, Son and Holy Spirit. We call it the Trinity. The word *our* in the creation account tells us there was a fellowship of love, peace, and eternal glory among the three persons of the Trinity. God is a relational being and throughout Scriptures it is apparent that he has a never-ending desire to connect with humans. Our God is a God of relationships.

Because humans were created in the likeness of God, we understand this relationship thing. In my men's Bible study we were asked, "Look back over your life. What's been most important to you?" These seasoned Christian men went around the table sharing what had the most value in their lives. No one chose belongings or stuff of this world. The greatest joys were people: spouses, children, grandchildren, friends. But some of our greatest disappointments, hurts, rejections, and failures were also connected with people.

Beginnings, fellowship, and relationships are part of God's story. This helps us better understand how grace was present before the beginning of this world.

Love produces more love

Love was present before the creation of the world. The night before he died for us, Jesus prayed, "Father, I want those you have given me to be with me where I am, and to see my glory, the glory you have given me because you loved me before the creation of the world" (John 17:24). The Apostle John was peering into a mysterious time before creation sharing an important characteristic about God. We do not know much about God in that time, but one thing is clear. Jesus, the one who loved us first, was first loved by the Father.

God's love is never ending. Present even before the beginning of the world, it is real and endures. The eternal love the Father had for the Son led to more love. The Father has a great love for people. This is demonstrated in that he sent his only Son as the Savior of the world. We are proof of God's enduring love.

A heart designed by God

Louis Washkansky was a simple grocer living in Cape Town South Africa. As a young man he was physically active in sports, but late in life his health deteriorated to the point where he suffered from congestive heart failure. Doctors determined that it was incurable and Louis found himself in a hopeless situation.

In 1966, at the age of 53, he met Dr. Christian Barnard who offered a glimmer of hope. Dr. Barnard gave him the opportunity of being the recipient of the first heart transplant. His only hope of living was an untested surgical procedure. Imagine his thoughts as he and his family talked through the decision-making process.

He opted to have the surgery. Even though he died 18 days after the operation, the surgery was considered a success because the new heart actually worked in Louis' body.

What would life be like if we did not have a heart? I'm not talking about the fist-sized organ that sustains physical life. The other "heart" is more difficult to describe. Although it includes our emotions, intellect, and will, it envelopes much more of our being. We can describe it as our personality, but it drills down deeper to the very nature of what makes humans, human. God in his infinite wisdom created men and women "in his own image" (Genesis 1:27). We are complex beings.

What does "image of God" mean? Adam and Eve had great intellect. Their cognitive ability enabled them to know what God wanted them to know. Their every desire and compulsion was in tune with God's will. Their emotions centered on serving God, and they knew what pleased him. They found great happiness in being able to love God, their creator. Their will was centered on serving and loving God. They were human imitations of what God is like. Their hearts encompassed this and even more. This heart idea was part of God's creation.

Men and women are God's capstone of creation. We are his greatest handiwork. The heart he gave us allows us to love and demonstrate emotion. It enables us to make good and pleasing choices, but also gives us the ability to reject, even our Maker. It provides the avenue for God's love to flow through motivating us to love others. The thanks we give him by our actions, including our gifts, praise him and show him love. The human heart sets us apart from the animals God created.

Through the heart God gives the capacity for us to love and to be loved. Every human is a unique heart-created being.

Corrupt from the beginning

If you are a parent, you remember the first time you held your son or daughter. Newly born babies look innocent, flawless. Their small bodies with miniature features are so wonderfully pieced together it is hard to comprehend that they began as a few cells several months before birth. Their tiny arms and legs wiggle just enough to indicate they are connected and functional. Even their needs are simple: feed me and keep me dry.

Oh, how wrong this picture is! "Surely I was sinful at birth, sinful from the time my mother conceived me" (Psalm 51:5). Every innocent looking baby of this world—including all past, present, and soon-to-be—are sinful, corrupt.

Corrupt. What a strong word! But it is true because God says so. Our corruption is an impurity from head to toe, a deviation of God's original design. This sin-corruption is beyond our understanding. Some may think it is simply a mistake, but it is more than that. Coming from sinful parents, we are so corrupt we cannot even understand how corrupt we are.

At one time Adam and Eve understood the opposite of corruption. They walked this earth without sin and lived in the image of God. They focused on praising God and serving him. One desire changed all of that. Maybe it was greed or a wanting to be like God or putting themselves first. Whatever! It was the first sin. Eve ate from the Tree of the Knowledge of Good and Evil and gave some to Adam.

God said "Don't!" yet they did.

Then their eyes were opened. They were naked, ashamed, and corrupted.

By all rights the God who issued the command to not eat the fruit could have—should have—destroyed them on the spot. Instead he called them out from their hiding, "Where are you?"

The God, who created grace before the beginning of time, now began to share that grace with mankind. He talked with them. He still loved them. Welcome to grace!

God, however, did tell them about consequences. Food would require work; work would be a challenge. Giving birth would hurt—a lot. Sin and selfishness would affect relationships between men and women. Conflicts caused by self-centeredness would enter relationships. Death would come and human bodies would return to dust. Painfully, Adam and Eve were banished from the garden so no one would be able to eat from the tree of life, which gave everlasting life. Grace was also found in God's response.

Whose idea was grace?

Grace was God's idea. It began before the creation of the world, the once-upon-an-eternity beginning. Grace is part of God's make-up, a key characteristic of an almighty God. From a human perspective, it is so simple it doesn't make sense. Once sin entered the world, grace followed because our God is a God of grace.

Grace entered this world "in the beginning." His never-ending grace keeps on coming millennia after millennia, century after century, year after year, and day after day. God's grace continues—even in eternity. God, our Father, relentlessly shares the grace that reaches more and more people—including you and me. Even "though outwardly we are wasting away, yet inwardly we are being renewed day by day" (2 Corinthians 4:16). God does not quit.

What a wonderful story! Just like it has no beginning, it is a story that has no ending. God's story is comprised of eternal bookends—and we are sandwiched in between. We are men and women, boys and girls, who have discovered God's grace. This is a story of love, relationships, and eternal beginnings. This is God's story, a story for you and me.

DIGGING DEEPER

Discuss

Humans are social beings. Our lives are filled with relationships. Think of connections you have made over the past five, 10, or even 30 years. God gives and treasures these relationships. Discuss insights of our God's relationship trait.

Loneliness can be one of the greatest crosses to bear. Humans tend to feel we can do it alone. However, we need each other, we need to belong. That is how we were created. Talk about the hurts (conflict, death, rejection) that come from loneliness. How can these be overcome by focusing on God's grace?

The Father loved his Son before the creation of the world. Sending him to this earth to live and die required unbelievable love. If you know someone who is struggling with life, how can you use these facts to encourage him or her?

Humans have one unique characteristic from all other creatures on earth: a heart once created in the image of God. How does this change your perspective of God? Of the people around you? Of you?

Our bodies are slowly wasting away. One day those bodies will be gone. However, the soul, the "inward" part, is renewed through hearing God's Word. Talk about the importance of being daily connected with God's Word.

Pray

Heavenly Father, you are the creator of grace. We are so thankful that you chose us to know about this grace. Because you want a relationship with us, we are now your children. Thank you for sharing your grace with us. Grant us the power to reflect your grace in our lives to everyone we meet. Bless our relationships so that your love is central. Amen.

Changed by Grace

We all regret wasted years from different seasons of our lives. They are vividly etched in our memories. Our shameful past is littered with poor choices, wounded relationships, and hurts. We have let others and God down. Yet God is still present. He answers with one word: grace. His story continues.

I have lived over five decades, and I realize how little I understand about God's grace, how little I appreciate it. How can God take me back time after time, mistake upon mistake? Do I really understand his never-ending love for me?

Maybe you can relate. We are short-sighted humans who have not fully grasped grace. We sing about it in a hymn, hear our pastor apply it in a sermon, read about it on a church sign, and say it is amazing. The Bible uses grace over 300 times and shares numerous stories that illustrate its impact upon the lives of people. It causes no trouble nor demands any commitment. But grace does require something. We can't earn it, but it costs us our lives.

What is the meaning of grace? How does grace impact my life? These are essential questions. Even more important are the hard-to-find answers. We forget to think about who we are or why we are on earth. Like two bullet trains passing by each other, life becomes a blur. The busyness of our day-to-day activities and the distractions of materialism cause us to lose focus. Sin and corruption have clouded our view of life.

We gloss over the deeper meaning of grace and do not personalize it for our lives. We do not grasp reality.

God does. God in his infinite design and never-ending passion of wanting all to be saved continues to give his grace, daily without fail, in ways we do not know. It changes our lives. Grace is a foundational component of a Christian's life.

Grace was God's idea, a part of his story. Now, it is part of our story. The two types of grace found in God's Word impact the lives of the Christian. They have a profound effect on the soul, mind, and heart.

Life-saving grace

God's judgment is true and final. When he tells us that "all have sinned and fall short of the glory of God" (Romans 3:23), his Word hurts and brings us down. When we think we can make up for failures or provide excuses for our sins, God says "there is no one who does good, not even one" (Romans 3:12). No one is excluded and everyone falls short. It is like running a race with a never-ending finish line. God knows our reality, and gives our story hope.

Grace demonstrates God's wonderful attribute: he wants to see everyone in heaven. One pastor I know has a special insight to God's passion. He told me that as he drives down the street he sees burning homes. "Huh?" I thought. He continued, "The people in these homes are headed to hell. Eternal fire waits. God called me to share the good news of Jesus with them."

God "is patient with you, not wanting anyone to perish, but everyone to come to repentance" (2 Peter 3:9). We are God's passion. He loves us. He is crazy about us. He can't stand the thought of spending eternity without us.

Sometimes, though, God's love comes to us differently. In the Old Testament, a truth leaps off the pages: God threatened *and* punished the people he loved. Adam and Eve's first sin had a consequence. A corrupt society was given time to repent; they didn't and a flood destroyed everything on earth—except eight humans and plentiful pairs of animals.

Time after time the children of Israel rejected God by worshiping idols, complaining, doubting, and arguing. God punished them for their sinful acts. By carrying through with his threats, God demonstrates how deadly sin is. However, God never does it with glee. Our God "does not willingly bring affliction or grief to the children of men" (Lamentations 3:33). He always shows grace, his love, to people.

Having known God since childhood, I do not remember what it was like to be an unbeliever. My father, however, clearly remembers what it was like to be an unbeliever, heading to hell. Then Jesus came into his life. I once asked him why he did what he did for the church and Jesus. His reply reflected his passion for God: "Growing up I never went to church, my parents didn't teach us about Jesus. Before I married your mother she encouraged me to study the Bible to learn more about Jesus. I learned how Jesus died and loved me even though I didn't know him. He came for me, and now I know him."

God's passion in seeking my dad was a lifelong change agent. Despair turned into hope. Dad's story is like yours.

The world won't recognize this amazing passion. His love and his grace are very different from anything in this world. He went to great lengths to demonstrate his love—and Jesus is proof. Our lives, even the past twenty-four hours, show we have not loved him back. We are rebellious, sinful to the core, and have rejected his commands in so many ways. Yet, God still loves us and seeks us out. His passion keeps coming, all because of his grace.

To discover grace is to uncover God's relentless love and steadfast passion for you. "For it is by grace you have been saved, through faith—and this not from yourselves, it is the gift of God—not by works…" (Ephesians 2:8). Did you catch that grace is a gift, totally free without any strings attached?

We did not want this grace, we did not deserve this grace, and of course we cannot earn it. It is all God's work. He did not ask us to climb a peak, but he came down in the valley and plucked us out. God provided the means. Grace, a gift from God!

God's relentless passion—wanting all humans to be saved—is the first type of grace. It is the manifestation of God's love. We are justified by his grace so that "we might become heirs having the hope of eternal life" (Titus 3:7). Grace gives our story deep meaning.

Life-living grace

Grace has a second meaning. In Scripture God tells us that grace is a gift, quality, or virtue that God gives to his people. The first grace—saving grace leads to more grace—grace for living.

When Paul wrote to the Corinthians about Christian giving, he said it was grace that moved them to give so cheerfully and generously. "And God is able to make all grace abound to you, so that in all things at all times, having all that you need, you will abound in every good work" (2 Corinthians 9:8). Paul uses the words "all" and "every" when giving encouragement. The same grace that gave them life eternal through Jesus was now working in their lives, powering them to do good works. God's abounding grace found in Jesus motivated the Corinthians to not only give generously ("whoever sows generously will also reap generously" v. 6), but also cheerfully ("for God loves a cheerful giver" v. 7).

Paul said it was "by the grace of God I am what I am, and his grace to me was not without effect . . . the grace of God that was with me" (1 Corinthians 15:10). The grace found in Paul was a continuous gift empowering him to do great things for God's kingdom. God caused his grace to flow through Paul much like fluids flow through a pipe. You and I are not buckets for storing God's grace. Instead, we are human pipes, letting his grace flow through our words and actions.

God's grace empowers people to do amazing deeds. Giving can be like that. Paul wrote "about the grace that God has given the Macedonian churches. Out of the most severe trial, their overflowing joy and their extreme poverty welled up in rich generosity" (2 Corinthians 8:1,2). Persecuted believers with few resources were generous givers because of God's grace. That's the power of God's grace!

God's grace teaches us to live godly lives filled with integrity and goodness. "For the grace of God that brings salvation has appeared to all men. It teaches us to say 'No' to ungodliness and worldly passions, and to live self-controlled, upright and godly lives in this present age . . . eager to do what is good" (Titus 2:11-14). The law tells us we should say no to ungodliness and worldly passions, but it cannot bring true obedience. God's grace provides the will, the strength, and the influence to change our lives. God's grace impacts our hearts. Once the heart is changed, lives are changed.

God's grace also comes into our lives as spiritual gifts. "We have different gifts, according to the grace given us" (Romans 12:6). God freely and independently dispenses them when, where, and to whom he pleases. We acknowledge our gifts and use them for God's glory and for the good of his kingdom here on earth.

God pours out his grace to believers, his grace-receivers. Grace is intertwined in our life story. We are saved by grace and live grace-filled lives.

Grace happens

God's story includes a never-ending supply of grace for you and me. "From the fullness of his grace we have all received one blessing after another" (John 1:16). The words "blessing" and "another" in the Greek are very similar. It literally means we get "grace instead of grace." Once grace comes, then grace comes again, and again, and again.

Grace is also always automatic for God's children. Sometimes when I walk into an unfamiliar, dark room, a light automatically comes on. I do not know how a motion-mechanism functions. All I know is if I walk into a dark room, light appears. God gives us grace in a similar way. We do not have to flip any switches to get grace. God supplies it to meet our needs. How that occurs, we do not know. Grace simply happens because of a God who loves us.

Grace is also happening *now*. I can't change me. But God is changing me into the image of Christ, from the inside out. Grace comes not because we have done good works, but so we can do them. Grace flows not because we deserve it, but because it is a gift. The best thing about this change is it is happening now, and will happen in the future. All because our God is a living God whose grace is always present and never-ending.

This always-present grace impacts our life stories in three ways: pardon, peace, protection.

- **Pardon.** This is the saving grace that wipes our sins away. You and I have eternal life because of what Jesus has done. Grace forgives our sins. When God looks at us he only sees Jesus' perfect life, not our sins! We are exonerated and eternal life is ours.

- **Peace.** Because we are redeemed children of God, we have no fears. God is on our side giving us his love. If times are tough, grace gives us contentment. When we sin, grace forgives us. If unhealthy thoughts come into our brain, grace replaces it with Jesus. If hurts come into our lives, grace soothes us. If we are sad, grace gives us joy. Grace gives us a full life, one of joy and integrity. Peace comes to us in ways we do not realize all because of God's grace.

- **Protection.** Do you wonder how many times the guardian angels have saved you from accidents? Even when our own stupidity can bring us harm, grace jumps in to save the day. It supports us when we are frightened. It calms our heart. God will always win the day for his people. Having protection on this earth is part of God's grace.

God's grace permeates our every moment of existence. That was God's intention from the beginning. We were designed to live daily with the sustaining help of God's grace. We may feel we can manage on our own, but without God's kindness, we are incapacitated. Our circumstances, troubles, and challenges simply are too much to handle on our own. It is by God's mercy alone that we are able to continue day after day. Our stories move forward in time.

Just like a motion-sensor light, I have no idea how grace works, but I trust and rely on it. If I use grace, more takes it place to use another time. No matter how hard I try, I cannot exhaust the supply of God's grace. In fact, I do not always realize when grace comes into my life. That is part of God's plan too. We are sustained in so many ways during so many times, it has become expected for the believing Christian.

God's grace powerfully infiltrates our life story. It gives us the power to both receive love and share that same love with our God and others. It gives us eternal life, and empowers our lives for living out that grace. Should we think of grace as a noun, a something? Or, is it more of a verb, an action? Grace came to us in the past, but we live it in the present. Don't get bogged down thinking too much about these questions. Grace happens. Now. Always. It connects God's story with our story. Believe it, live it, and rejoice over it!

DIGGING DEEPER

Discuss

Talk about the statement: Reality is how God views life.

God has a deep passion for humans. He loves us and is so crazy about us. How does this fact help propel you forward in life?

Think of a time when some level of anguish entered your life (loss of a loved one, hurt relationships, financial struggles). Because of God's love and compassion, your anguish turned into hope. Share the circumstances of this time and how God lifted you up out of the valley of despair.

Paul's words in 2 Corinthians 9:8 have deep meaning: "And God is able to make all grace abound to you, so that in all things at all times, having all that you need, you will abound in every good work." How do the words "all" and "every" give encouragement for your giving financial gifts to gospel ministries? In your response, use the analogy that we Christians are more like a pipe than a bucket.

Like an automatic motion sensor light, God's grace provides pardon, peace, and protection every day. Talk about what that means for you in living your life.

Our life stories are evidence that God and his grace are at work in our lives. Explain how God's continued grace paves the way for a bright future.

Your Story, a Reflection of God's Story

If your childhood was anything like mine, you probably learned the value of sending some kind of "thank you" acknowledgement after receiving a gift. Such a simple act is a part of what is called good manners. Recognizing a gift from another is a wonderful thing and deserving of a grateful response.

God gave and still gives grace. We respond in various ways. For our purposes, we focus on one response, Christian giving. Although giving is our response, God has a plan for it. Whenever God gives instructions on giving, whether Old Testament or New, the heart is involved. God understands that our heart's actions energize our response. Our response is our story.

God and our hearts

God knows that our heart's transformation gives us a stronger loyalty toward him, a more passionate desire to serve and praise him. Ezekiel uses a word picture when he prophesies about the transformation of Israel and their hardened hearts: "I will give you a new heart and put a new spirit in you; I will remove from you your heart of stone and give you a heart of flesh. And I will put my Spirit in you and move you to follow my decrees and be careful to keep my laws" (Ezekiel 36:26, 27).

Don't you love that picture? God is interested in heart transformation. By giving us a heart of flesh, he also gives a desire to follow his will and commands. God initiates the change, which gives us comfort and assurance as he works in us.

Do you believe you live *for* Jesus or does Jesus live *in* you? There is a major distinction between the two. The answer impacts your story. It all begins with the story of how God the Father and Son are one. When Jesus prayed to the Father the night he was arrested asking for unity of all believers, he stated, "I in them and you in me" (John 17:23).

The fact that the Father is in Jesus makes it possible for Jesus to be in us. On another occasion Jesus encourages believers to "remain in me, and I will remain in you" (John 15:4). To complete the unity circle, the Apostle John reiterates the same thought but expands the truth to include the Holy Spirit. John writes about Jesus living in us. "Those who obey his commands live in him, and he in them. And this is how we know that he lives in us: We know it by the Spirit he gave us" (1 John 3:24).

Recall God's wonderful story of love, grace, and fellowship before the creation of the world. His story was of three persons: Father, Son, and Holy Spirit. That story continues today. Upon our conversion, God took our old heart and replaced it with a new one. Now Jesus does live *in* us. When we understand that truth, then we live *for* Jesus.

My new heart is the heart of Jesus inside me. That aspect of the heart transplant is God's grace too. Grace has given us the heart of Jesus that lives for Jesus!

Learning to live with our new hearts is a constant battle. Our sinful desires often revert back to our old heart. Our old self pushes Jesus aside. It enjoys the indulgences of this world, its pleasures and treasures. Sometimes the old heart wants us to give up, lose interest, grow bored, seek novelty, or be guided by our head only. Learning to live with our new heart takes a lifetime because our old heart wants to reject the transplant.

Jesus is our anti-rejection medication. By staying connected to Jesus through the Word of God, we have a steady stream of God's grace. God's grace then flows through us to others.

Two functions of faith

Faith affects our ability to live Christ-filled lives. Our heart is at the center. In our faith life-story two functions impact daily living for Jesus.

The first function, saving faith, is when the Holy Spirit causes us to believe that through Jesus' perfect life, we have life eternal. Ephesians 2:8 tells us "you have been saved." Because of God's grace, our salvation is complete through faith in Jesus. The confidence that we will one day be in heaven is because of our "saving faith" found in Jesus and nothing else. It is a fact. Those who believe this fact have faith and are assured that heaven is theirs!

The second function of faith, trusting faith, moves us to action. "Faith by itself, if it is not accompanied by action, is dead" (James 2:17). The Holy Spirit moves us to do God's will *and* also empowers us. True faith produces good works. No good works, no faith. These works are good in God's eyes and always come from authentic trusting faith.

Our trusting faith increases when we are connected to Jesus, to the Word. An example of increasing faith is found in your personal offerings. Think back to earlier years when you first began giving gifts to the Lord. Compare that with your current giving. Even factoring out inflation, my guess is that your giving to gospel ministries has increased. The older you get, the more you understand God's care for you.

An increase in offerings, which decreases the money for yourself, reflects your trusting faith. Jesus commended the centurion from Capernaum by saying, "I have not found anyone in Israel with such great faith" (Matthew 8:10). That great faith believed his servant would be healed simply by what Jesus said.

When a furious storm came upon the disciples in a boat and they thought their lives were endangered, Jesus said, "You of little faith, why are you so afraid?" (Matthew 8:26). They were afraid of losing their lives and forgot to trust God's providence. Trusting faith as given by the Holy Spirit empowers us to be productive followers in every facet of our life, including giving that is powered by grace, *grace giving*.

God's grace found in saving and trusting faith are at the heart of being committed believers who desire to glorify God. Powered by the Holy Spirit, our daily living, which includes our grace giving, is a reflection of our faith.

Giving engages the heart and mind

Our giving story continues. Giving is not just involving the heart, it also engages the mind. These two processes, heart and mind, are connected and flow out of the faith of the believer. Paul told the Macedonians that each should give "what he has decided in his heart to give" (2 Corinthians 9:7).

The first process is an exercise of the mind. We analyze our current giving, begin to establish benchmarks, and then identify the portion of our income we plan to give. Before a decision is made, we think about the amount and type of gift, and reflect on how the plan will unfold in our lives. Finally, a giving plan emerges that guides a response. In most instances, our brain provides the rationalization for a giving plan.

The second process of giving is a commitment of the heart. Fully committed believers take the time to consider their role in God's kingdom. Who am I? What is my purpose here on earth? How might God be asking me to invest in his kingdom? How has the Lord blessed me?

The real measurement of trusting faith is not the size of our offering, but the size of our heart. A heart enlarged by grace and filled with Jesus' love empowers believers to grow in the percentage, the amount, or the future plans for giving. People give as they believe, not as they are able.

Giving joyfully

The familiar passage, "for God loves a cheerful giver" (2 Corinthians 9:7), can be a challenge to understand. God loves those who give joyfully, but what about those who do not give with joy? Does God not love them? How do I know if I'm giving joyfully? What does it feel like? What really is God's purpose for focusing on the heart of those who give? The question that begs to be answered: Why does God love a cheerful giver?

Perhaps this passage can best be understood with an analogy. Picture parents with a newborn. Relatives and friends come up to the proud parents and comment on the features and how they resemble the parents. The parents beam. You see, when others identify features of their baby and associate those features with the parents; it is a reflection of the parents.

The same is true of God. Our God is a giving God. He first gave us this wonderful planet. He also gave us Jesus, his one and only Son, to die on a tree for our sins. He continually gives us what we need each and every day without fail. God gives and gives even without our asking, and that is the connection between God loving a cheerful giver and us. When we give and imitate a giving God, God smiles. He is praised because we are imitating him. When God sees his children giving joyfully and generously, he sees himself in us. He sees Jesus in us.

God himself is a cheerful giver. He made the world based on the plan of cheerful giving, and the great Artist loves to see his plan imitated. There is no grudging in his compassion. If he shows mercy, he delights in mercy. If he gives, he gives with open hands and a smiling face.

So, is your giving really *cheerful*? Christian giving is a freedom of choice. Husbands, what if your wife informed you that from now on she was to receive a box of chocolate candies every Friday. That would be your way of showing your love for her. And, by the way, if a box of chocolates does not appear, terrible consequences will follow. How would you react? My guess is that very soon this act would become old and tiring. Still you would give out of fear, all to avoid the trouble. Giving would be a chore because you didn't have a choice. The gift is more like a payment to keep your wife happy.

That kind of giving is law dominated, with a demand or sense of obligation attached to it. It simply is not connected with the heart. Acts of true love are centered upon a choice. Wives appreciate it when husbands give thoughtful, unexpected gifts. God wants gifts that are *our* idea in an amount that reflects our appreciation for what he has done.

God long ago wiped away any rules as to how much we are to give him. He looks forward to givers who reflect his love. The Greek word for "cheerful" is used only once in Scripture. It means to have "won over" or "already inclined." It describes someone who is cheerfully ready to act because they are already persuaded to give. Our English word "hilarious" comes from this word. It is a spontaneous, non-reluctant giving that exudes joy. It reflects a get-to attitude rather than a have-to.

Cheerful givers enjoy giving. It is a reflection of God's grace in the giver's heart that produces such fruitfulness. God loves it!

Living urgently

If you have been to a hospital emergency room during a crisis you have seen what it looks like to live with urgency. As patients come in they are sent through a process called triage. This means their needs are assessed and placed in one of three categories – will survive without treatment, will not survive with treatment, will survive with treatment. Those in the last category are treated first. All decisions are made on the basis of need. Factors such as wealth, fame, and power have no bearing on determining need.

We live in a busy society. As the years go by, life gets more complex. Sometimes it feels like we are living in a hospital emergency room overrun by patients. Busyness makes us lose focus on the important things in life. Our heart can become attached to things of this world, unbalancing our life.

Imagine that you were given insider information: Jesus is coming back in one year. How would your life change? My hunch is that you would be more focused. You would be more vocal about sharing Jesus with others. You would live more urgently.

Now a follow-up question: how would your giving change? If Jesus were coming next year, all earthly things would become worthless once he arrived. We cannot take any of the things from this world to heaven with us. No one has ever seen a moving van following a hearse.

When Jesus comes, our money will become worthless. It is kind of like the Confederate currency one year before the Civil War ended in 1865. If you owned a lot of Confederate dollars and knew the war was going to end, it simply would be foolish to hang onto that money. Within a year's time, they would not be worth anything at all.

This is just like today's greenbacks, the dollars in our bank accounts and those we use to buy cars, homes, stocks and other "needs" of life. Soon, they will be worthless also. Jesus said not to count on those things "where moth and rust destroy, and where thieves break in and steal" (Matthew 6:19).

As Christians get older, this sense of urgency becomes stronger. We gain a deeper Biblical perspective on life and its meaning.

In the past my mother loved to buy and collect old things. Our home and garage were packed full of antiques and collectibles. It got to the point that she opened a store in order to reduce her treasures. This act also provided an excuse to buy even more! That was almost four decades ago. Now, for the past several years she continues to downsize. First it was moving into a 700-square foot apartment. Then, it was a constant stream of selling or giving things away. Now, it seems like every time I visit her, she is giving something else away. The reason: "I have to give it away! I don't need it and it is not going with me."

Mom has a deeper perspective on why she is living on this side of heaven. It is not for gaining more things and building up a money portfolio. It is living for Jesus with a sense of urgency. Jesus will be coming for us soon and, when he does, things of this world will no longer have any value. Our new hearts long to see Jesus face to face!

Grace demands a response

Grace begs a response to the one whose heart understands. Once grace has come into a person's heart, responses follow. There is a saying: Billiard balls react, but people respond. When a person grasps the great lengths God has gone to seek them out, there can only be praise. Our sins are forgiven, God declares us sinless. We respond. That is our story.

Grace is a gift. Period. We did not earn it; we can never think of earning it. Humans deserve to be declared guilty, but God declares us righteous because of what Jesus has done. Forgiveness for our sins is God's gift to us through the perfect life of Jesus. Grace is given not because we have done any good works. No, grace is ours so that we can do good works.

Our good works—a thought, word, or action of praise—flow from thankful hearts. God produces good works in believers whose lives are dedicated to Jesus. God's Holy Spirit creates a powerful new life in each believer. Through his work in us we daily demonstrate good works.

Just as a tree produces fruit, so the new life the Holy Spirit has created in us propels us to do good works. A response is made. The Bible calls it the grace of giving.

I worked with a pastor and his leadership team in developing concrete financial goals for a funding emphasis. A goal was proposed that was rather lofty. The eyes of the team gave away the doubts floating around in the room. Finally someone spoke up, "What if we do not reach our goal?" Heads nodded in unison.

Their pastor responded with appropriate words to this possibility. He said, "Any time a Christian gives, it is a good thing."

When God's people give, *grace giving*, it is a good thing. God's grace propels us to give. The roots of our giving go back to God's story from the beginning. Our story is a response to his story.

DIGGING DEEPER

Discuss

God gave all Christians a heart transplant. Through grace the heart of Jesus lives in us, and now we live for Jesus. Talk about your transplant and how that impacts your life.

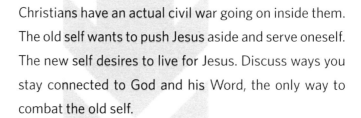

Christians have an actual civil war going on inside them. The old self wants to push Jesus aside and serve oneself. The new self desires to live for Jesus. Discuss ways you stay connected to God and his Word, the only way to combat the old self.

Christian giving engages both the heart and mind. Think of some of your past gifts or giving plans. Share with the group how your heart and mind worked together in giving a gift or planning for a gift.

Gods says that he loves a cheerful giver. Some may question whether or not they are joyful when giving a gift. True, lasting joy comes from a solid source, "for the joy of the LORD is your strength" (Nehemiah 8:10). Describe the comfort this passage gives to you.

On the following blank, name one thing found on this earth that you will take to heaven: _____.
Assuming the blank is still blank, talk about the lasting value of those things that you currently call your own. How can this perspective impact your giving?

The Stories

A Story About Stories

God's grace is lavishly abundant. That understanding of God's grace in our lives would pass us by completely should we choose to focus on the things of this world. God's grace is real. It is part of your life story—right now. As you walk through life, may God open your eyes more clearly to his wonderful grace and include a generous response to it.

Stories stick with us. Perhaps you remember listening to your grandparents' stories. My Grandma Elsa told stories about my mother and her siblings, and of the grandfather I never knew. Grandma's stories always captured my attention and communicated her life's wisdom.

The storyteller's background and years of experience color the theme, and give truth to the lesson. They are captivating because they are real.

The following stories focus on grace giving. They show how God's people responded in heartfelt praise for the many things God has done. They reflect God's never-ending, always-flowing grace. They are stories of how God's love moved them to love. They are encouraging heart stories.

The writer of Hebrews states, "let us consider how we may spur one another on toward love and good deeds" (Hebrews 10:24). The word "spur" is an interesting way to describe this encouragement. The

Greek literally means to "arouse or excite, to call into action." Our actions and words can excite others to love and perform good deeds. Love, the basis of all beautiful deeds, is the purest and mightiest inspiration. The following stories illustrate love in action and spur others in their every-day living.

Yet these aren't grand stories, they are simple, grace-filled stories. They are true, though some are a compilation of several smaller stories. So sit back and enjoy some quick reads.

If you are part of a group, coordinate the story reading and meet face-to-face as a follow-up. The Digging Deeper sections are a way to enrich the story and connect with your daily living for Jesus. Discover how God's grace impacted lives and motivated others to follow and imitate Jesus. Whatever your role—mother, father, son, daughter, congregation leader, supporter, encourager, or simply a "giver"—follow God's grace and grow. May he bless your journey as you respond to his grace.

Giving Story

Anna
a generous giver

Joyful Christian Giving

And now, brothers, we want you to know about the grace that God has given the Macedonian churches. Out of the most severe trial, their overflowing joy and their extreme poverty welled up in rich generosity. For I testify that they gave as much as they were able, and even beyond their ability. Entirely on their own, they urgently pleaded with us for the privilege of sharing in this service to the saints.

2 Corinthians 8:1-4

In his grace, God gives Christians the gift of giving and the freedom to express that gift.

Anna is more than ninety years old. She loves her Lord and she loves her church. When there is a need, Anna always does her best.

After one Sunday service, the chairman of the congregation talked to the congregation about our growing deficit. Anna called me during the week and asked me to come over. She gave me an envelope containing 50 twenty dollar bills. She said she always put one $20 bill aside during the week so she would have something in case there were extra doctor bills, or her furnace broke down.

"But," she said "the church is more important."

Paul did not hesitate to tell the Macedonians about the collection for the needy saints in Jerusalem, even though he knew how impoverished they were. If he did tell them, he certainly didn't push for their participation. He didn't have to. They pleaded with him for the opportunity to give.

The result was a welling up of "rich generosity" on their part. That's not a good translation of the word, though. It literally means a "singleness (of purpose)." Giving to the Lord gave them so much joy that they would rather give than eat. Wouldn't you love to have that kind of spirit? Wouldn't you love to have such joy in giving that nothing else really mattered as much?

Actually, you already do. The same Spirit that put faith in your heart also gave you a singleness of purpose regarding the Lord and his work. That spirit of generosity—or that singleness of purpose—may be lying dormant. It may need some cultivation and encouragement from God's Word. But it is there. God's grace is in you.

I sometimes wish I could only share the needs of the church with those who aren't impoverished. So I'm glad Anna is there to remind me that giving isn't only for the wealthy. Knowing Anna's heart, she wouldn't want to miss out on the opportunity to give to her precious Lord and his work. How about you?

Thanks be to God for this indescribable gift!

DIGGING DEEPER

Concepts:

grace ✦ rich generosity ✦ joyful giving ✦ singleness of purpose ✦ freedom

Ask:

In what way do both the poor and the rich have an equal opportunity to give to the Lord's work?

Discuss how opportunities to give offer us an opportunity to examine our singleness of purpose?

Think of people who have been excellent examples in the grace of giving. Share their stories. What made them such good examples?

Study:

Read Mark 12:41-44. Jesus wonders at the singleness of purpose shown by a widow's offering. Discuss the widow's attitude.

Pray

Pray: Lord Jesus, when an opportunity to give to others is presented to us, send us your Spirit to fan into flame this gift of generosity that you have put into our hearts. Amen.

Me and My Bicycle

Grace Powers Us Forward

Someone in the crowd said to him, "Teacher, tell my brother to divide the inheritance with me." Jesus replied, "Man, who appointed me a judge or an arbiter between you?" Then he said to them, "Watch out! Be on your guard against all kinds of greed; life does not consist in an abundance of possessions." And he told them this parable: "The ground of a certain rich man yielded an abundant harvest. He thought to himself, 'What shall I do? I have no place to store my crops.' "Then he said, 'This is what I'll do. I will tear down my barns and build bigger ones, and there I will store my surplus grain. And I'll say to myself, "You have plenty of grain laid up for many years. Take life easy; eat, drink and be merry."' "But God said to him, 'You fool! This very night your life will be demanded from you. Then who will get what you have prepared for yourself?' "This is how it will be with whoever stores up things for themselves but is not rich toward God."

Luke 12:13-21

God's grace gives the power to overcome our old self as we fight the battle between hanging onto things of this world and letting go by looking forward to the next world.

I remember purchasing my first bicycle. It was a bright yellow 10-speed with curled handlebars. I had saved up for it doing various jobs over several months. Though it was years ago, I remember how much is cost ($110) and where I bought it (our local hardware store). On top of that, it was a Schwinn, one of the finest bikes a boy could buy. It was my pride and joy, something that a 12 year old can understand. I saved, and I got. It was mine.

Then it happened. As I was riding home from a friend's and crossing a busy street, I rode in front of a car. A trip to the hospital in the ambulance was the end result. Fortunately, I was not seriously injured. The same could not be said of my shiny yellow Schwinn. It was totaled. I was heartbroken. But I learned a valuable lesson: things of this world do not last.

Today, our "shiny yellow Schwinns" may be massive, many-square-foot homes, large portfolios comprised of stocks and bonds, life-styles that exceed the average, or so much stuff that we rent storage space to contain it.

Jesus talked about a "Schwinn" owner. A farmer collected barns, so many that he filled them up and had to order new ones. His life would soon to be over and he would leave his "Schwinns" behind. His greed made him focus on things of this world, which were not in sync with God's will.

Perhaps you can identify. Are you held hostage by something of this world? Do you own some stuff that in actuality owns you? We cannot get enough money, possessions, and security. The sin of greed makes finding the right balance between getting and giving a daily struggle. Jesus knew that, and warned against it.

Jesus calls believers to be faithful managers. Our heart's attitude impacts our decisions as managers. God's grace allows us to redirect things of this world toward gospel ministries and helping the poor. His grace flows through us when we give, and give generously. His grace allows us to combat the greed that can overtake hearts.

DIGGING DEEPER

Concepts:

> greed ◆ old self vs. new self ◆ covetousness ◆ management ◆ happiness

Ask:

> We have filled our homes and garages with things our heart craves. Name three items that actually list (binding agreement) you as the owner. Explain how this is a contradiction. Describe (be specific, please) what will eventually happen to those items.

Discuss: The more you accumulate and oversee as a manager, the more demands you have. Giving is the antidote to accumulating stuff. Explain the tension between managing and giving.

Jesus is not condemning riches in this story. He is condemning a wrong attitude toward riches. Identify ways we can become rich toward God.

Study:

Luke 12:22-31. After the Parable of the Rich Fool, Jesus talked about not worrying. The rich man was not properly prepared for the future. Discuss how the right priorities help put our lives in perspective. Thinking of contentment and worry, what will you spend your time thinking about today?

Pray:

Lord Jesus, at times we mix up our priorities and live for the present, for the things of this world. Give us your strength daily to fight the desires of the old self. Replace those desires with love for you and what you did for us as well as what you do for us. Refocus our hearts on things above and fill them up with the assurance of your love. Amen.

Giving Story

I-Just-Want-to-Know Bart

God's Grace, Our Motivation

For you know the grace of our Lord Jesus Christ, that though he was rich, yet for your sakes he became poor, so that you through his poverty might become rich.... For if the willingness is there, the gift is acceptable according to what one has, not according to what he does not have. Our desire is not that others might be relieved while you are hard pressed, but that there might be equality.

2 Corinthians 8:9, 12, 13

God's love for us, because of Christ, motivates us to give from the heart in order to meet the needs of others.

When I teach a new-member class, I try to be thorough when talking about Christian giving. We talk about giving in response to what God has done for us. We talk about giving God the first-fruits of our labors. We talk about including giving as part of our family spending plan.

Bart was a young, successful businessman who was planning to join our congregation. Lesson after lesson, I watched him mature in his faith. He asked lots of questions, often making our class last longer than usual. Bart made a conscious effort to put his faith into practice. If I suggested family devotions, he started them. If we discussed ways to pray, he tried them. He was a human sponge.

I tried to give him all the tools he needed to make giving decisions that would honor the Lord. But he wasn't satisfied.

"Pastor," he said, "I respect your judgment. You know about how much I make. Tell me how much I should give each week."

We reviewed the principles of giving again.

"You don't get it," he said, "I want you to tell me exactly how much I should give!"

When I said I couldn't do that, he became angry. Finally, I said, "Bart, if I told you how much to give, I know you would give it. But I want you to think about it, pray about it, and then think some more and arrive at your own decision. Because when you do that, God has more than just your dollars. He has your heart!"

In the New Testament God does not tell us how much to give. Paul spent all of 2 Corinthians 8-9 on this subject. Does he ever tell the Corinthians exactly how much they should give? No. He used phrases like "according to your means." When you read these chapters it makes you pray and think and wrestle to arrive at a decision that will honor God.

But Paul is explicit about the motive of our giving. "For you know the grace of our Lord Jesus Christ, that though he was rich, yet for your sakes he became poor, so that you through his poverty might become rich" (2 Corinthians 8:9). We give because of grace. We give because Jesus died to give us the wealth of heaven.

So pray and plan and wrestle as you think about what you will give to your Lord. Call to mind his promises and what he has done for you. Then the Lord will have something really special from you—your heart.

DIGGING DEEPER

Concepts

grace ◆ rich-poor contrast ◆ Jesus, motivation ◆ heart

Ask:

Old Testament people were required to give a "tithe." What principles from the law of the tithe in the Old Testament are helpful for us in the New Testament?

Identify some less-than-godly motives for giving that our old self can come up with. Share some teachings or ways you have used to overcome these motives?

Why do you think God is so interested in our heart when we give a gift to honor him?

Conclude the story. What should Bart have done?

Study:

Read Luke 18:9-14. Contrast the Pharisee's motive for giving with that of Paul's when he describes Jesus becoming poor so that we can be rich. How is Bart like a Pharisee? How is he not like a Pharisee?

Pray:

Lord Jesus, you became poor so that I might be eternally rich. Use me, Lord, and all that I have—my treasures, my time, and my talents—to give you glory now and always! Amen.

Geese Lesson

Leaders Need Encouragement

As for Titus, he is my partner and fellow worker among you; as for our brothers, they are representatives of the churches and an honor to Christ. Therefore show these men the proof of your love and the reason for our pride in you, so that the churches can see it.

2 Corinthians 8:23-24

God's representatives use his Word to encourage his people to grow in the grace of giving.

Talking and preaching about money had never been a problem for me. My internship year, my supervising pastor trained me well, teaching me to talk about stewardship and giving. I learned to present God's grace as you teach giving, people respond.

Now I was at a new church. Ten months ago, when I became the pastor, the president made it clear that giving was a priority. To move forward with the ministry plans of the congregation, they needed a steady growth pattern. Increased giving was part of the plan.

As pastor of this flock, I worked with sub-committees, connected with individuals, and garnered the support of the church leadership. In response to a flat-line of giving over the past several years, we drafted the next emphasis for Christian giving. Today I was presenting the plan to the largest group of the congregation.

The meeting with the church leaders seemed to be going nowhere fast.

As each goose flaps its wings, it creates uplift for the bird following. By flying in a "V" formation, the whole flock adds over 70 percent greater flying range than if the bird flew alone.

As the discussion continued into its second hour, I began to feel the effects of the weeks of hard work. Very few were enthused about giving. There was no sense of urgency. Many felt it was the preacher's job to do this task. Yes, I felt responsible for taking the lead in developing a plan. Looking back, I did the majority of work, but now, I was presenting the plan and feeling quite lonely.

**When the lead goose gets tired, it rotates back into the flying forma-
tion and another goose flies at the point position.**

I began to hear excuses phrased as questions. Why can't those
who are not giving begin to give? Who can give more dollars in this
economy? Why does the church have to always talk about money? Ob-
viously, many incorrectly thought the solution was someone else's problem.

One person said, "We will never be successful."

Others nodded. Someone added, "This is just another gimmick
to get people to give more to the church."

I was becoming frustrated.

**The geese in formation honk from behind to encourage those up front
to keep up their speed.**

Once again I tried to explain how important this topic is for
Christians. Living in the country that we do, it is easy to let wealth and
possessions become our god. Our heart wants to please our old sinful
desires of greed and envy instead of living for Jesus. Jesus had a lot to
say about money and possessions. He knew in every age of the history
of this world, the struggle with money would need addressing.

"Our focus in this church should be on something other than
money."

**When a goose gets sick, wounded, or shot, two geese drop out of for-
mation and follow it down to help and protect it. They stay with it until
it is able to fly again or it dies. Then they launch out on their own with
another formation, or catch up with the flock.**

As the meeting broke up, I sank heavily into my chair, wondering how I would challenge God's people to grow in the grace of giving.

DIGGING DEEPER

Concepts

encouragement ✦ trust ✦ leading ✦ following ✦ yearly giving plans ✦ encouragement ✦ teamwork ✦ representatives ✦ Christ-led.

Ask:

Your pastor (lead goose) can teach Christian giving in a variety of ways: annual appeals, sermon applications, Bible studies, and encouraging estate planning. What steps might put a stronger focus on giving for your church?

How do other leaders (geese) support and encourage the pastor to be bold, creative, and faithful in preaching and teaching about Christian giving?

Paul calls the representatives who are going to gather the offering "an honor to Christ." The Greek literally means, "the glory of Christ." Their character reflected something of the brightness of Christ's beauty and glory. How are your leaders like these representatives?

Paul urges the Corinthians to open their hearts to his representatives. He tells them, "Show these men the proof of your love." Paul exhorts the Corinthians to demonstrate their love for these brothers who were coming to help them. What might your words and actions look like when your pastor and other leaders begin talking about money, encouraging you to give generously?

Study:

God understood that money would be an issue for all ages. God's design for collecting money is unique among organizations in our country. Read 1 Corinthians 16:1-4 and identify principles for first-fruit giving (gifts that are the first and best) for God's people.

Pray:

Dear Lord, there have been many times that I have not adequately supported our pastor and leaders, especially when they talk about money. Encourage them to move forward in these areas to challenge God's people in Christian giving. Open my heart to hear the words you want me to hear. Amen.

Giving Story

Carol
a testimonial giver

Glorifying God Though Giving

This service that you perform is not only supplying the needs of God's people but is also overflowing in many expressions of thanks to God. Because of the service by which you have proved yourselves, men will praise God for the obedience that accompanies your confession of the gospel of Christ, and for your generosity in sharing with them and with everyone else.

2 Corinthians 9:12-13

God assures us our generosity will cause others
to glorify him.

A letter came from Carol's power of attorney. Carol is one of
our shut-ins at the care center. She is not so old, but arthri-
tis has crippled almost every joint in her body. She never married. She
owned a farm once, but that's gone with the cost of her care. It's a joy to
visit her. She always greets you with a smile. She never complains, even
if you squeeze her hand too hard.

The letter contained a donation of $500 for the church. Her at-
torney included a note, "In all likelihood, there may not be future pay-
ments on her behalf. Hopefully, this will provide satisfaction to her and
comfort her in knowing she made an effort. I have not visited with her on
this. In all likelihood, unless time permits, I will not be informing her as to
this contribution. So should you comment on it during one of your visits,
she may not comprehend."

What struck me is that Carol's generosity has always been so
evident that someone took it upon himself to make a gift from her estate
without her knowledge. He did it, not to satisfy any need or request the
church expressed, but because he knew that giving would "provide satisfaction and comfort to her." Giving made Carol happy. Even her lawyer
knew that!

There are so many people in our churches like Carol, or like the
Macedonians in Paul's day. They give because it is a joy to give. They
give in spite of their poverty. They beg for the opportunity. By their giving
they show their single-hearted devotion to the Lord and to his church.
They have been blessed by God with the grace of giving.

I wish I could say I've always been such a shining example of
Christian charity! I've been less than joyful in giving. ("Why are they al-

ways asking for money?") I've treated giving as a burden. ("Why do I have to be the one who gives more?") What am I saying about my love for Jesus when I feel that way? What example do I set when I express those feelings?

I know that God who is rich in mercy has forgiven all my sins. He accepts the generous gift I've given without joy. He accepts those I've given out of a sense of duty rather than from a pure and thankful heart. For Jesus' sake, he accepts those given some with pure and some with not-so-pure motives. God will continue to work in my heart so that someday my giving will cause others to glorify God for the work he has done in me.

DIGGING DEEPER

Concepts:

generosity, giving ◆ glorifying God, ◆ joy ◆ testimony ◆ praise ◆ proven

Ask:

Discuss how parents or grandparents can teach their children the joy of giving by example.

Talk about the difference between giving being a burden versus a joy opportunity. How has your view changed over the years?

Talk about how the church today might acknowledge people's gifts. How can this be done to give glory to God?

The word "proved" in 2 Corinthians 9 has the idea of successfully passing a test. It was used to describe coins that were genuine and not counterfeit. How does this apply to your life as a grace giver, a living and breathing Christian?

Carol's life demonstrated that giving was a major focus of her life. How does this happen in your life?

Study:

Read Philippians 4:10-20. Paul thanks the Philippians for their continued generosity. What can we learn from these passages?

Pray:

Lord Jesus, you have been good to us in so many ways! Give us that grace, too, so we give with joyful and generous hearts. When we give, guide us in setting an example for others and give glory to you alone! Amen.

Giving Story

My Dreams on Giving

Contentment Brings Spiritual Happiness

But godliness with contentment is great gain. For we brought nothing into the world, and we can take nothing out of it. But if we have food and clothing, we will be content with that. People who want to get rich fall into temptation and a trap and into many foolish and harmful desires that plunge men into ruin and destruction. For the love of money is a root of all kinds of evil. Some people, eager for money, have wandered from the faith and pierced themselves with many griefs. But you, man of God, flee from all this, and pursue righteousness, godliness, faith, love, endurance, and gentleness. Fight the good fight of the faith. Take hold of the eternal life to which you were called when you made your good confession in the presence of many witnesses.

1 Timothy 6:6-12

God wants us to be content in his promises and to share earthly wealth so others may believe and be saved.

When the lottery gets over 100 million dollars, I dream of winning. Now, I do not buy lottery tickets because I would rather put one dollar in my children's college account than waste that dollar on a dream. But that doesn't stop me from dreaming of finding the winning number in the store's parking lot.

I imagine all the good things I would do with all that money. I would build new classrooms and a gymnasium at our area Christian high school. An endowment fund would enable our congregation to start a Christian elementary school. Funding ten new mission congregations a year for the next ten years—done! Sometimes a new vehicle for the family enters the picture. But most of the time my dreams are quite innocent, almost sanctified.

Maybe you have similar dreams. But are they really so sanctified? "But godliness with contentment is great gain." The fact is that God has given us all that we need for our personal happiness, and for carrying out the work that he has set before us in this world. If we are lacking in anything, we can be confident that "God will meet all your needs according to his glorious riches in Christ Jesus" (Philippians 4: 19).

True happiness is not found in our dreams of winning the lottery. It comes through Jesus Christ. It's rooted in the gift of eternal life that is ours without cost. It grows as we apply his promises to every aspect of our lives. It shines through us as we live simple, joyful, and godly lives.

God's work is not accomplished by our dreams of winning the lottery. It's done when I open my mouth and tell my neighbor about Jesus. It's done when I carefully manage what God has given me and use it to feed and clothe my family. It's done when I set aside a portion of what

I have for sending a missionary into the world, or for building the addition onto our Christian school.

The next time the lottery is over 100 million, I pray I will be content with what God has given me to use. Besides, up until now, my dreams haven't really accomplished anything.

DIGGING DEEPER

Concepts:

contentment ◆ rich ◆ wealth ◆ love ◆ need ◆ wants

Ask:

Write down your dreams. Are they rooted in reality?
How do you assess whether you are content with what
you have?

Why is the "love of money" and not just "money" the
root of all kinds of evil? What evil can come from loving
money?

True happiness comes from sharing Jesus with others. This may come by our words (personal testimony) or by our giving to gospel-based causes. Share some happiness stories you have experienced.

Discuss the difference between a want and a need. One song writer penned, "All that I have is all that I need." Identify some Scriptural principles from this quote.

Study:

Read Ecclesiastes 5:10-20. Why does worldly wealth not satisfy? What things give lasting satisfaction?

Pray:

Lord Jesus, let my dreams be rooted in the reality that true joy and contentment is found only in you and in your righteousness. Amen.

Giving Story

Tiny
the basketball player

Material Wealth is a Blessing from God

Command those who are rich in this present world not to be arrogant nor to put their hope in wealth, which is so uncertain, but to put their hope in God, who richly provides us with everything for our enjoyment. Command them to do good, to be rich in good deeds, and to be generous and willing to share. In this way they will lay up treasure for themselves as a firm foundation for the coming age, so that they may take hold of the life that is truly life.

1 Timothy 6:17-19

Jesus wants us to instruct his people, and especially those who have been blessed with material wealth, regarding the Christian management of money and the spiritual gift of giving.

I remember the day I got cut from the freshman basketball team. I was so angry! I knew I wasn't great. But I imagined that I was a lot better than the coach thought I was. What really irked me was they kept someone who couldn't even make a lay-up! He couldn't shoot well. He couldn't dribble. He couldn't handle the ball. The only thing he had going for him was that he was big. He was really big!

I watched from the sidelines that year as the coaches worked with this big kid who couldn't shoot. First they taught him how to do lay-ups. Then they showed him a better way to shoot. They taught him where to play offense and how to play defense. They even taught him how to rebound—as if he needed any! With patient instruction, the big kid became a good player.

The next year I did make the team. I got a chance to show my stuff. But the big kid was always a little better. To be honest, he was a lot better. Because he had one thing I didn't have. He was big.

Being rich is like being big. It's a blessing that God gives to some people and not to others. He does not make them rich because he loves them more. He does not make them rich because he loves them less. Some have this gift because God has showed them how to work hard and invest wisely. Others have this blessing because they were born into a wealthy family.

Being rich is like being big. It gives you potential. When you see a fellow human being in need, you can do something. When you see an opportunity for sharing the gospel, you can make it happen. Because your income far exceeds your needs, you can do what most people only dream of doing for the kingdom of God.

But like the big kid on the basketball court, you need to learn how to handle yourself so your life and your wealth glorify God. God has made you rich in a more important way. That's why he gives us his Word, and pastors, teachers, and Christian friends to coach and encourage us. God's Word is our light on our journey through life. It shows us how to live—and how to give—all to the glory of God.

DIGGING DEEPER

Concepts:

> wealth ✦ rich ✦ generous ✦ sharing ✦ God's glory

Ask:

> How would you define "wealthy" by yearly income? By
> accumulated savings? Now define wealthy by spiritual
> standards.

> What kinds of special instructions should we give those
> who are rich? How can we better share those instruc-
> tions?

How do you consider yourself rich? Explain.

Make a list of all the daily gifts that make life both possible and good. Which are truly necessary? With respect to material goods, view the list one more time and assess your level of contentment versus discontentment.

Study:

Read Luke 7:1-10. How did God use the Centurion's wealth to benefit the kingdom? The faith of the Centurion was very great. Even Jesus said so. Discuss the concepts of wealth, faith, trust and giving.

Pray:

Lord Jesus, you have blessed this generation with great wealth. Our country is so blessed. Now give us the wisdom to use our worldly wealth to your glory and honor. Never let it become as important in our lives as the riches we have in you. Amen.

The Giving Story

Giving Story

Lenny
loved by God

An Example for Loving Christian Leaders

I thank God, who put into the heart of Titus the same concern I have for you. For Titus not only welcomed our appeal, but he is coming to you with much enthusiasm and on his own initiative. And we are sending along with him the brother who is praised by all the churches for his service to the gospel. What is more, he was chosen by the churches to accompany us as we carry the offering, which we administer in order to honor the Lord himself and to show our eagerness to help. We want to avoid any criticism of the way we administer this liberal gift.

2 Corinthians 8:16-20

Above all, the administration of Christian giving is a spiritual activity and can be carried on with confidence by the spiritual leaders of God's church.

Lenny was in his 80's and dying of cancer. In a roundabout way, I was invited to minister to him before he died. He had been baptized and confirmed in our church. Why had he left? He told me a chilling story. When he was thirteen years old, his father died. There was little support for his family. Lenny brought in a little money through odd jobs, but in that first year, there wasn't much even for food and clothes.

Lenny and his mother were in church the day the treasurer of the congregation read the list of those who were behind in their church "dues." If someone gave nothing at all that year, his or her name was read and the amount listed as nichts—nothing. When Lenny told the story, you could hear the sneer in the treasurer's voice. After he was confirmed, Lenny never returned to the church that had shamed his mother.

Over 60 years later, I was grateful that God gave me a chance to minister to Lenny before he died. I spoke to him of his spiritual needs. He forgave others.

I was thankful for the reminder that in a Christian congregation, Christian giving should be administered by spiritually-minded people whose greatest concern is the heart of the giver. Such leaders will set the tone for the congregation and keep giving on a spiritual level, where it belongs.

"As he looked up, Jesus saw the rich putting their gifts into the temple treasury. He also saw a poor widow put in two very small copper coins, 'I tell you the truth'" he said, 'this poor widow has put in more than all the others. All these people gave their gifts out of their wealth; but she out of her poverty put in all she had to live on.'" (Luke 21:1-4). Perhaps Jesus had seen such a woman shamed as well. And he wanted to set the record straight. God's greatest concern is the heart of the giver.

That's why Paul speaks of his concern for the Corinthians, not just the offering for the saints in Jerusalem. That's why Paul sent them a spiritually-minded man like Titus. When Christian giving is administered by spiritually-minded people, mistakes like the one that offended Lenny rarely happen.

Those who administer the grace of giving in a Christian congregation share God's love for the giver.

DIGGING DEEPER

Concepts:

> love ◆ Christian giving ◆ reporting ◆ heart ◆ law and Gospel motivation

Ask:

> Reading names of people and how much they gave is an example of using the law to shame (or build up) Christians into giving. Identify other ways you have seen the law used to "motivate" people into giving.

> Why can it be so difficult to discuss money in the church?

How can we do a better job in our church of honoring the gifts, large or small, of all God's people?

People often say, "My giving is between me and God." What may be the reasons for such a statement? Explain how this statement is both true and untrue.

Study:

Read John 12:1-11. Jesus defends the extravagant gift of a woman whose heart was in the right place. She trusted God completely for all of her future needs. How is this an inspiration and model for your giving?

Pray:

Lord Jesus, grant us to be sensitive to the hearts of your people whenever we encourage them to give generously. Guide us, above all, to be concerned with their spiritual growth and welfare. Amen.

"Rich" Emma

A Different Type of Giving

For you know the grace of our Lord Jesus Christ, that though he was rich, yet for your sakes he became poor, so that you through his poverty might become rich.

2 Corinthians 8:9

Through financial planning, God's grace provides the motivation to give to ministries even after people enter heaven.

Emma was a 78-year-old widow and a life-long member of her church. She taught Sunday school, sang in the choir, served in the women's group, and always had kind words for everyone. Her time management and service to God's kingdom was exemplary. Emma's husband, Leroy, recently passed away. He was just as active as his wife and loved his church and Lord very much. He now was singing praises to Jesus in heaven.

Emma's three children, plus the wonderful eight grandchildren, are mature, financially stable adults. Their chief concern is for mom's financial security and well-being. Emma owns her own home and has some modest financial investments. Leroy's pension and Social Security benefits provide Emma with a comfortable living.

Recently, Emma told some friends at church that she wanted to sell her house and move to a retirement center. One of her friends said that the church's planned giving committee could help make plans. Emma immediately made contact.

Her desire was to make a gift in Leroy's memory that would help the church and not leave her financially stranded. Creating a Leroy Memorial Fund within the church endowment account seemed like a good idea. Emma and Leroy both had a passion for outreach in the community and foreign mission fields. The endowment would allow her to gift yearly income to both causes.

Emma was presented with two options to fund the endowment. The first was to create a charitable remainder trust. The trust could be funded from the proceeds of the sale of her home and set up with the church's foundation. Each month or quarter the foundation would send her a check to use however she wished, as long as she lived. Upon her death, whatever is left in the trust would go to the church's endowment fund. Emma could spell out exactly how she wanted the income to be used, including funding other ministries.

The second option was something called a charitable gift annuity. Emma could receive income for life to use however she desires. Again, upon death, the final proceeds are given to the church's ministry. In both options a lawyer is needed to take care of legal documentation and other paper work.

Emma felt good about exploring both options and moved forward with her choice. She was thankful that Jesus gave up so much to come down from heaven to take away her sins. This type of earthly planning was a way for her to say "thank you, Jesus."

These types of estate planning tools, as well as others, allow those who may not have much in terms of earthly wealth, to give substantial gifts to their local church upon death. These people are currently faithful givers, but wish to give even more upon death. It is yet another way to leave behind a legacy of faith.

Emma is a grace giver. She understood a grace truth: the one who was rich became poor so she could become rich.

DIGGING DEEPER

Concepts:

>   planned giving ✦ wills ✦ endowments ✦ poor-rich com-
>   bination ✦ foundations ✦ legacy

Ask:

>   During certain times of life people may be more willing
>   to discuss estate planning options. Below are some key
>   opportunities for pastors to encourage thoughtful dia-
>   logue. What other occasions may be added to the list?
>   Why might these times be called "trigger points" for
>   planned awareness?
>
>   - Couples preparing for 2nd marriages
>   - Parents preparing for children's dedication/baptism
>   - Death of a spouse
>   - Visits with aged and shut-in members
>   - Health crises and funeral planning
>   - Receiving new members, especially from out-of-
>   state
>
>   Identify your congregation's current efforts in promot-

ing Christian estate planning awareness and education. What more can be done?

In 2 Corinthians Paul refers to Jesus as being rich then becoming poor, so that the readers of his letter can become rich. Discuss each phrase:

- "though he was rich"
- "he became poor"
- "you through his poverty might become rich"

Study:

Christian giving centers on our response, motivated by love, for what Jesus has done. Read Romans 3:21-26 to refresh your memory of this wonderful fact.

Pray:

Dear Jesus, your great love drove you to this earth to suffer and die for our sins. At times we forget this fact and do not appreciate its true meaning. Bless us with a fuller understanding of your great love and guide us to give out of love for what you have done for us. Amen.

The Giving Story

Giving Story

"Get to" Erin

Living for Opportunities

After this, Jesus traveled about from one town and village to another, proclaiming the good news of the kingdom of God. The Twelve were with him, and also some women who had been cured of evil spirits and diseases: Mary (called Magdalene) from whom seven demons had come out; Joanna the wife of Cuza, the manager of Herod's household; Susanna; and many others. These women were helping to support them out of their own means.

Luke 8:1-3.

Followers of Jesus have the opportunity and privilege to invest in gospel ministries that support the work of Jesus.

Erin's church was having a capital campaign to raise money to build an addition. The leaders focused on the spiritual aspect of the decision making process. Their emphasis was not on the raising of dollars, but rather the raising of hearts. Erin, a young mother, was serving on the leadership team.

We were studying another Bible lesson on Christian giving and nearing the end of the discussion. The group was deep in reflection mode when Erin finally said, "I get it. It is not about a 'have to', but a 'get to'."

I asked her to explain what she meant. "Well, when we give it should not be something that we *have to* do, but rather something that flows from a joyful heart. When I think about giving, it is all about my opportunity to give back to my Lord. I *get to* do this thing we call giving."

"Get to" versus "Have to." The latter focuses on motivating the old self, and quickly becomes a law-dominated reason for giving. Giving becomes an obligation—a have to, a must do.

Did you ever wonder how Jesus supported himself during his three-year ministry? It appears Jesus was not gainfully employed. Because he called the disciples away from their income producing careers, they were not working either. Here we have a group of men who went from town to town listening to Jesus preach and teach about the good news of salvation. So, how did they support themselves?

The reading from Luke tells us. A group of women were following Jesus and supporting him with their resources. Some of the women were named; a greater number are recorded as "many others." The women who crisscrossed the countryside with Jesus supported him. They had a "get to" attitude.

That is a good picture of the work of our gospel ministries today. "Many others" represent all who give on a regular basis. You and I are not following Jesus aimlessly, but with purpose. Our gifts, large and small, support God's kingdom. The time we invest in ministry also supports the work of the Lord.

"Many others" are you and me today. Praise God we "get to." Thanks, Erin, for your get-it-done attitude!

DIGGING DEEPER

Concepts:

opportunity ◆ investing ◆ service ◆ men / women giving

Ask:

What are the similarities between the women in the reading and today's givers in our churches?

The phrase "many others" can describe those who give of their time and treasures in today's churches. Explain how this phrase has special meaning for you.

The Bible verses in this chapter recognized people and their giving. Mary, Joanna, and Susanna were highlighted. Other givers were anonymous. Our new self needs no recognition for the giving of a gift. Our old self, however, is different. What are some good reasons to recognize givers?

Can leaders say "thank you" too much?

Besides the important thank you letter, identify other ways to recognize grace-filled givers?

Study:

Read Acts 4:32-37. Barnabas means "encourager." Through our giving we can encourage others to live a joy-response life. What are reasons why our giving God may have placed this story in his Bible?

Pray:

Dear heavenly Father, you have entrusted us with wealth beyond our thinking. Thank you for blessing us in so many ways. You also have given us the opportunity to support your many and varied ministries here on earth. Give us the strong desire to invest in these ministries so more can hear of your Son, Jesus. Amen.

The End or is it... the Beginning

Every story is supposed to have a conclusion. Well, maybe not *every* story. Because our faith continues to grow, our Christian giving is always growing, never ending.

Our life story is a series of events, one after another. Our experiences mesh with our faith to produce results. The following activities are intended to guide the believer in producing heartfelt gifts.

Use them to reflect upon your past story. Let them propel you forward in new ways of giving. Be inspired to live each day out of thanks for what our God has done.

Our life story is a living, breathing reflection of God's grace. So, your life story continues. As you create new stories, may God's grace continue to motivate you to do great things for his kingdom!

A Generosity Autobiography

Your story about giving

What is your story? Thinking through past giving habits can help you better understand yourself. More importantly, it points you forward.

Jot down some notes in the following categories and talk them over with your spouse, partner, or friend. Share your past giving stories as well as the hopes and dreams of the future. Your responses will help you better understand your life and giving. Pray that God continues to bless your generosity in the months and years to come.

- **Family history:** How did your parents teach you about giving? What events or decisions had a major impact on your viewpoint of giving? How did mom or dad give to others? To the church? To other causes?

- **Personal history:** Trace the path of your giving to other organizations. What is one of the earliest or most vivid recollections about giving money? How has your giving grown over the years? What giving opportunities have been good? Which have been surprises, good or bad? Who is or was the most financially generous person you know?

- **Present case:** What is one of the biggest things you've learned about generosity from this study? What truth or Bible verse stood out the most? What new spiritual perspectives or insights did you discover over the past several weeks?

- **Future plans:** Describe how God is working in your life in a fresh way because of a change in your attitude or a change in your giving? How will this study influence your giving to your church, other ministries, or special needs? Do you have new goals or plans for generosity?

Your Turn, Your Story

How Much Should I Give for the Lord's Work?

Wouldn't it be nice if the church just sent us a bill once a month and told us how much we should give? Like our electric or phone bill, we wouldn't have to make a choice on how much to give. We would simply know what was expected of us.

Christian giving does not work that way. What we give to the Lord is a choice each of us makes. Our decision is a response to God's love for us and becomes part of our grace story.

How do I decide what to give to my Lord?

Go to God in prayer and ask for his guidance. Your heart will be touched. Then, engage the mind and give thoughtful consideration to a giving amount. This agrees with 2 Corinthians 9:7:

> *Each man should give what he has decided in his heart to give, not reluctantly or under compulsion, for God loves a cheerful giver.*

- Step A

  What percent do I want to give for my church?

  My goal is _____%

- Step B

  Calculate the yearly giving amount by multiplying the above percent times your total family income. This figure represents your planned yearly gift.

  My yearly total giving is: $_____

- Step C

  Make it doable by dividing the total yearly giving amount by the giving period, week(s) or month(s). This determines your "giving habit."

  I/we plan to give $_____ every _____.

- Step D

  Rejoice and give thanks that God has allowed you to not only set up a plan for giving, but will provide the means for you to do so. Pray regularly for the Holy Spirit to move you in following through with the giving plan.

  Yes, I acknowledge that God is the ultimate owner of everything I manage. I commit to the above giving plan for the Lord's work. I trust that God will supply me with all that I need. This plan of action will begin within one week from today.

_____   _____

signature   spouse's signature (if applicable)